TAYLOR SWIFT

REAL BIOS

by Marie Morreale

Children's Press®
An Imprint of Scholastic Inc.
New York Toronto London Auckland Sydney
Mexico City New Delhi Hong Kong
Danbury, Connecticut

Photos ©: Alamy Images: 30, 31, 43 top (AF archive), 11 (BWAC Images), 20 (Wenn Ltd); AP Images: 24 bottom (Evan Agostini), 18 (Mark Humphrey), 14 (Rex Features); Corbis Images/Splash News: 29; Dreamstime: 15 top right (Drugoy66), 43 bottom (Gary Lewis), 40 top (Sbukley), 15 bottom left (Showface); Everett Collection: 13 center; Getty Images: 8 (Al Messerschmidt), 21 bottom (CBS Photo Archive), 38 bottom, 39 bottom (Christie Goodwin), cover (Christie Goodwin/TAS), 2, 3, 4, 5, 36 (Christopher Polk/ TAS), 6 background, 7 background (Dave Hogan/TAS), 25 top (David Krieger/Bauer-Griffin), 44 (Erika Goldring), 21 top (Ethan Miller/ACM2009), 9 (Frazer Harrison/ACM2009), 23 (Keith Bedford/Starbucks), 1 (Kevin Mazur), 34, 35 left (L. Cohen), 10 (Larry Busacca), 22 top (Michael Loccisano), 35 right (Michael Ochs Archives), 25 bottom (Michael Tran), 38 top, 39 top (NBC), 12 (NCP/Star Max), back cover (Nicky Loh/TAS), 28 (Scott Barbour/TAS), 13 bottom (Taylor Hill); Newscom: 7 (David Mills/Splash News), 42, 43 left (inffr-01/INFphoto.com), 26 (infusny-231/Paul Adao/INFphoto. com), 13 top (Sasha, CelebrityHomePhotos), 22 bottom (Shirley Perkins, PacificCoastNews), 17 (snitcherdesk/Splash News), 15 bottom right (Splash News/Keds), 24 top, 32 (Tom Donoghue/Polaris); Rex USA/Matt Baron/BEImages: 41 bottom; Shutterstock, Inc.: 40 center (cinemafestival), 15 top (ecliptic blue), 40 bottom, 41 center (Helga Esteb), 6 (Robert Elias), 15 center top, 41 top (s_bukley).

Library of Congress Cataloging-in-Publication Data
Morreale, Marie.
  Taylor Swift / by Marie Morreale.
    pages cm. — (Real bios)
  Includes bibliographical references and index.
  ISBN 978-0-531-21376-6 (library binding) — ISBN 978-0-531-21429-9 (pbk.)
  1. Swift, Taylor, 1989– —Juvenile literature. 2. Country musicians—United States—Biography—Juvenile literature. I. Title.
  ML3930.S989M67 2015
  782.421642092—dc23[B]   2014031113

Taylor brought her Red Tour to Detroit on May 4, 2013.

MEET TAYLOR!

AMERICA'S SWEETHEART SHINES

Taylor Swift—singer, songwriter, icon. At just 25 years old, she has sold millions of albums, won a devoted audience of fans called Swifties, and become a role model the world over.

How did Taylor become one of today's most popular entertainers? Talent. Hard work. Daydreams. And mistakes. When *Glamour* asked what advice she would give herself if she could turn back time, she said, "I wouldn't change anything. I would repeat the same regrets, the same mistakes, the same wonderful, beautiful, accidental triumphs."

If you want to find out more about Taylor, check out her *Real Bio* story. It's Tay-rific!

CONTENTS

Taylor sends out music, love, and hugs to all her concert audiences.

TAYLOR SWIFT'S
FAIRY TALE

FROM A CHRISTMAS TREE FARM TO THE STAR ON TOP

Taylor Swift's story is practically a legend. Her parents, Scott and Andrea Swift, raised Taylor and her younger brother, Austin, on an 11-acre (4.5-hectare) Christmas tree farm in eastern Pennsylvania. Scott was a stockbroker, and Andrea was a former marketing executive. When their kids came along, they decided to move to the country. It was a fairy-tale atmosphere, complete with beautiful trees, a grape arbor, and seven horses. "I had the most magical childhood, running free and going anywhere I wanted to in my head," Taylor told *Rolling Stone* magazine.

Taylor has always been very close with her mom, who

Below: Taylor is joined by her family at a 2011 CMA event—(l. to r.) younger brother Austin; dad Scott; and mom Andrea.

Taylor's fave guitar is made by Taylor Guitars—no relation!

encouraged her to express her talents. "I think my earliest memory is my mom would set up an easel in the kitchen when I was three," Taylor revealed in another *Rolling Stone* interview. "And she'd give me finger paints and I'd paint whatever I wanted, and it was always good enough."

That kind of encouragement helped make Taylor who she is today. "[My mom] let me know I could do whatever I wanted with my life," Taylor explained to *Cosmopolitan UK* magazine.

Painting wasn't Taylor's only talent. She rode horses and eventually competed in shows on her mom's horse, Cinnamon Twist. She loved to make up fairy tales to share with her family. And, of course, she loved to sing—especially songs from Disney movies. "I was that annoying kid who ran around singing for random strangers," she laughingly told *CosmoGirl* magazine. "Music was always it for me."

Singing was definitely everything to Taylor, and she isn't embarrassed by how she got her first audiences. "I have been singing randomly, obsessively, obnoxiously for as long as I can remember," Taylor told *Marie Claire* magazine. "My parents have videos of me on the beach at, like, three, going up to people and singing *Lion King* songs for them. I was literally going from towel to towel, saying, 'Hi, I'm Taylor. I'm going to sing 'I Just Can't Wait to Be King' for you now.'"

> **"MY #1 CONFIDENCE TRICK IS: THROW YOUR SHOULDERS BACK!"**

Taylor was six years old when she heard a LeAnn Rimes album for the first time. The experience changed her life. She became a huge fan of country music, listening to LeAnn, Shania Twain, Faith Hill, and the Dixie Chicks constantly. When she was eight, she went to see LeAnn Rimes perform live. It was Taylor's first concert. After the show, she stood in line for hours to get her idol's

Taylor is thrilled to meet her first idol, LeAnn Rimes, in 2009.

autograph. "I was totally freaked out," she explained to *Philadelphia Style* magazine. "Seeing this person who was my hero . . . it was just crazy."

After watching a TV special about Faith Hill, Taylor learned that Nashville, Tennessee, was the center of the country music world. The first thing she did after the special ended was look up where Nashville was. Nine-year-old Taylor was determined to follow her dream. "I learned it was this amazing city where country music lived," she told *CosmoGirl*. "I was like, 'That's the promised land of country music. That's where I need to go!'"

Next, Taylor wanted to get some experience on stage, so she joined a local children's musical theater company. She loved performing, but she confessed to *Rolling Stone*

Another special moment for Taylor—meeting country music superstar Faith Hill.

that she actually preferred the cast karaoke parties. "Singing country music on that karaoke machine was my favorite thing in the world," she admitted.

Taylor took her karaoke kicks further. She entered local karaoke contests, and when she finally won, the prize was priceless. She got to open for legendary country musician Charlie Daniels! Taylor was in heaven. She was singing country songs and getting recognized for it. She even sang the national anthem at a Philadelphia 76ers basketball game. But unfortunately, this success also put the middle-school-age singer in another kind of spotlight.

Around that time, the Swifts moved from their Christmas tree farm to a suburb of Reading, Pennsylvania. Taylor had to go to a new school. She remembers being the ultimate outsider. "So . . . middle school? Awkward," she told *Vogue* magazine. "Having a hobby that's different from everyone else's? Awkward.

THE BASICS

Singing the national anthem on weekends instead of going to sleepovers? More awkward. Braces? Awkward. Gain a lot of weight before your growth spurt? Awkward. Frizzy hair, don't embrace curls yet? Awkward. Try to straighten it? Awkward. So many phases!"

And so many mean girls. "Middle school was what programmed me to be semi-insecure, like, all of the time," Taylor told *Vogue*. "I didn't fit in."

Taylor took to writing about her emotions. Mostly she wrote in her journal, but she had gotten into

FULL NAME: Taylor Alison Swift

NICKNAMES: Tay, T-Swizzle, Swifty

BIRTHDAY: December 13, 1989

CHILDHOOD HOMETOWNS: Cumru Township, Pennsylvania, and Wyomissing, Pennsylvania

SUMMER HOME: Stone Harbor, New Jersey

CURRENT PETS: Scottish Fold cats Meredith Grey and Olivia Benson

BEST FRIEND: Abigail Anderson—since ninth grade!

INSTRUMENTS: Guitar, banjo, piano, ukulele, electric guitar

EARLY MUSICAL INFLUENCES: Shania Twain, the Dixie Chicks, Britney Spears, Stevie Nicks, LeAnn Rimes, Kelly Clarkson

CAREER ROLE MODELS: Paul McCartney, Bruce Springsteen, Emmylou Harris, Kris Kristofferson, and Carly Simon

CURRENT HOMES: Nashville, TN; Beverly Hills, CA; Watch Hill, RI; New York, NY

FASHION ICON: Audrey Hepburn

FRAGRANCES: Wonderstruck and Wonderstruck Enchanted

LUCKY NUMBER: 13

GUILTY PLEASURE: Watching YouTube videos of kittens and using the CatPaint app—"I CatPaint all my pictures. It's weird."

FANS' NICKNAME: Swifties

TWITTER HANDLE: @taylorswift13

writing poetry early on. When she was in fifth grade, she wrote a poem called "Monster in My Closet." It placed in the top 10 in a poetry contest sponsored by a student writing organization called Creative Communications. And when Taylor was 12 years old, she wrote a 350-page novel!

Music was more important to her, though, and Nashville was her magic city. She had to go. At age 11, Taylor convinced her mom to take her to the Oz of country music during spring break. She started knocking on record label doors along Nashville's Music

FACT FILE

FAVORITES

"I WAS A TANGLED-HAIRED, BAREFOOT KID RUNNING AROUND ON A FARM FOR MY CHILDHOOD."

AT-HOME PASTIME:
Baking cookies—
pumpkin chocolate chip are her best

RELAXATION SPOT: Radnor Lake
State Park—"I've had some of my
best days walking there with my
dad, talking about life."

CHILDHOOD TOY: Beanie Babies

TV CHANNEL: The History Channel

TV SHOWS: Grey's Anatomy, CSI, and
Law & Order: SVU

CELEBRITY: Ellen
DeGeneres—"She's my
favorite person to talk
to. She brings out the
best in everybody."

BOOKS: "Anything
by Elizabeth
Gilbert!"—such as
Eat, Pray, Love and
Committed—and also
The Hunger Games and
To Kill a Mockingbird

COUNTRY SINGERS: Tim
McGraw, Kenny Chesney, Brad
Paisley, Faith Hill, Shania Twain

MOVIE: Love Actually

COLORS: Red, burgundy,
mustard yellow, and deep purple

BODY LOTION: The Body Shop's
Strawberry Body Butter

SUNBLOCK: Kinerase Daily Defense
Cream

LIPSTICK: Red

AFFORDABLE CLOTHING STORES:
Urban Outfitters, Anthropologie, H&M,
Forever 21, Target

NIGHT OUT: Singing karaoke

HOLIDAY: Christmas

PRECIOUS STONE: Opal

FLOWER:
Hydrangeas

SNEAKERS:
Keds—
she's the
spokesperson
for the brand

Row. There, she handed out CDs of some of her karaoke performances. "Hi, I'm Taylor, and I'm interested in getting a record deal," she told people as she gave them the CDs.

Unfortunately, the phone didn't ring when she returned home to Pennsylvania. Taylor didn't give up, though. "I realized that I needed to find a way to have a fighting chance of making it," she told *Teen Vogue*. "So I started writing songs and playing the guitar."

The first song Taylor wrote was "Lucky You." Taylor talked about it in a Scholastic "Read Every Day" live Webcast: "It was about this girl who's different. She believes in herself. It somehow got leaked online and it is a terrifying experience when people bring it up because I'm like, 'I sound like a chipmunk. I'm 12 in that.' But you look back on your first experience with writing and every one of those experiences turns you into who you're going to be."

Superpower Wish . . .
"To read people's actual thoughts!"

"Lucky You" was prophetic. Taylor was going to become a very lucky girl, indeed. But first she had to write more songs. Taylor had plenty of things to write about. "For the first time, I could sit in class and those [mean] girls could say anything they wanted about me,

In the studio, Taylor is totally involved with the song she's recording.

because after school I was going to go home and write a song about it," she told *Rolling Stone*.

When Taylor felt she had written enough songs to show that she was truly a singer/songwriter, she and her mom made several more trips to Nashville. Not only did she hand out CDs of her original work, but she also played music industry **showcases**. Important people began to notice her, and things started ramping up.

It wasn't a surprise when the Swifts decided to move to Nashville to support Taylor's new journey. At age 14, Taylor knew that she was where she was meant to be. "I just knew that I've never felt anything like the happiness and fulfillment I feel after I finish a song," she told *InStyle* magazine. "I was learning to say it the way I felt it."

In 2006, Taylor looks like the ultimate country singer.

TAYLOR MADE

COUNTRY . . . POP . . . AMERICA'S SWEETHEART

Just moving to Nashville didn't make Taylor an overnight success. She still had a lot of work to do. She had already made changes. She was writing her own songs. She had reached out to the Nashville music executives. The next move was to have the right people see her perform. The Bluebird Cafe is a Nashville legend. Many country singer/songwriters have been discovered there. Taylor was able to set up a solo showcase at the Bluebird. "Everyone showed up," she told *Allure*.

The audience was packed with music industry biggies who had the power to sign her immediately. But, as she looked out over the crowd, there was one man who was obviously listening and really hearing her. He had his eyes closed and swayed with Taylor's music. She knew he got it.

The man was a music industry veteran, Scott Borchetta. He

> TAYLOR GIFTED ED SHEERAN A HANDMADE NEEDLEPOINT WITH A QUOTE FROM DRAKE'S SONG "STARTED FROM THE BOTTOM."

had worked with several major music companies. At the time, he was setting up his own label, Big Machine Records. Taylor was one of the first artists with the new label. Borchetta knew that Taylor had talent as a singer and songwriter, but he wanted to introduce her to all the different areas of the music business. In 2005, Borchetta arranged for Taylor to be an **intern** at the Country Music Association (CMA) Music Festival. Her job was to escort the artists

"I WAS MORE SCARED IN JUNIOR HIGH THAN I WAS OF NASHVILLE."

around and make sure they made it to interviews and performances. Little did she know it would be only a matter of months before she would need her own escort.

Taylor's debut single was "Tim McGraw." Borchetta had Taylor and her family working hand in hand on the promotion. She went on a huge TV and radio tour to promote the song.

Taylor's Timeline

On the Road

OCTOBER 24, 2006
Taylor Swift is released

NOVEMBER 11, 2008
Fearless is released

JANUARY 10, 2009
Taylor is the musical guest on *Saturday Night Live*

FEARL
TOUR 2
PRESENTED

AMERICAN GREE
americangreetings

Taylor and manager Scott Borchetta win the 2009 CMA Album of the Year for *Fearless*.

Even when Taylor was home in Nashville, she wasn't resting. She remembered sitting on her bedroom floor with her mom stuffing envelopes with the "Tim McGraw" single to send to radio stations. She told *Billboard*, "With every envelope that I would seal, I would look at the address and the station on there and think, 'Please, please just listen to this one time.' . . . There's no promise when you're putting out your first single that people are even going to listen to it."

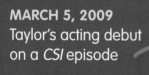

MARCH 5, 2009
Taylor's acting debut on a *CSI* episode

AUGUST 8, 2009
Wins two Teen Choice Awards: Female Artist and Album for *Fearless*

Taylor shows off one of her many CMA Awards.

In October 2006, Taylor released her first album, *Taylor Swift*. Taylor wrote three songs on the album and cowrote many of the others with country music songwriting icon Liz Rose. Not only did a lot of radio programmers and DJs listen to it, but so did a lot of country music fans. Eventually *Taylor Swift* sold more than 5.5 million copies worldwide. With her growing success, Taylor spent much of 2007 as the opening act for major country stars such as George Strait, Kenny Chesney,

NOVEMBER 7, 2009
Taylor hosts *SNL*

FEBRUARY 12, 2010
Taylor's first movie role in *Valentine's Day*

MARCH 27, 2010
Wins Nickelodeon Kids' Choice Awards: Female Singer and Song for "You Belong To Me"

Brad Paisley, Tim McGraw, and Faith Hill. That same year, Taylor earned one of the Nashville Songwriters Association Songwriter Artist of the Year awards. Taylor was the youngest songwriter ever to receive the award.

In November 2008, Taylor released her second album, *Fearless*. She wrote eight of the album's songs, including the smash single "Love Story," which introduced her to an audience beyond country music fans. Five of the other singles all charted. *Fearless* won Album of the Year and Best Country Album at the 52nd Grammy Awards. It also won an American Music Award, Academy of Country Music Award, and a CMA Award.

Taylor's third album, *Speak Now*, was released in October 2010. Taylor wrote all 14 songs, and she even coproduced the album. Declared by critics as her best

High Watch
Taylor's Rhode Island home cost almost $18 million.

AUGUST 9, 2010
Taylor wins four Teen Choice Awards, including Best Female Breakout for *Valentine's Day*

OCTOBER 25, 2010
Speak Now is released

AUGUST 7, 2011
Taylor wins six Teen Choice Awards, including the Ultimate Choice Award

to date, *Speak Now* showcased Taylor's very personal lyrics and musical growth. *Rolling Stone* called Taylor one of the best songwriters in pop, rock, or country. You couldn't walk into a store, turn on a TV, or listen to the radio without hearing Taylor Swift singing her heart out.

Red was Taylor's fourth album. It was released in October 2012. She wrote most of the songs herself, but one of her favorite collaborations was on "Everything Has Changed" with her new BFF Ed Sheeran. *Speak Now* had sold 1,047,000 copies during its first week. *Red* sold more than twice that amount in the same time! It

In 2014, Taylor was named Billboard's Artist of the Year for the second time.

DECEMBER 2, 2011
Billboard names Taylor Woman of the Year

OCTOBER 22, 2012
Red is released

MAY 19, 2013
Taylor wins eight Billboard Music Awards including Artist of the Year and Billboard 200 Album for *Red*

MARCH 10, 2014
Tops *Billboard's* 2014 Money Makers list

When Taylor loved Harry Styles . . . they took a walk in NYC's Central Park.

held the number one spot on *Billboard*'s Top 100 chart for more than two months. The album's singles—"We Are Never Ever Getting Back Together," "Begin Again," "I Knew You Were Trouble," "22," "Red," and "Everything Has Changed"—all hit the top or near the top of the charts.

Taylor was proud of her professional success, but would rather have kept her personal life revelations to her lyrics. "I don't really write for albums as much as I just write for my life and process what I feel, whether

AUGUST 18, 2014
"Shake It Off" video is released

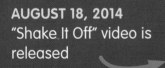

OCTOBER 10, 2014
Taylor becomes the first ever artist to be chosen as Billboard's Woman of the Year a second time.

OCTOBER 27, 2014
1989 is released and Taylor shoots right to the top of the pop charts

Taylor and one-time BF Conor Kennedy in Hyannis Port, MA

that feeling is resentment or hope or happiness or a crush—writing songs helps me get through those moments," Taylor revealed to *Rolling Stone*.

To Taylor, songs are diary entries, plays, and fairy tales all rolled up in one. Admittedly shy, Taylor finds that the best way to share her feelings with others is through her lyrics and songs. "I'm excited about telling the beginnings of stories, like the story of this song called 'Ours,' where I wrote about the guy nobody thought I should be with," Taylor told VH1 News. "So I wrote this song specifically to play it for him, just to show him, 'I don't care that you have a gap between your teeth. I love you for who you are.' And that song actually making it on [*Speak Now*] and is becoming a #1 song. . . . Songs happen in really weird, strange, quirky ways, and to explore the start of them, where they were first brought into the world, where you first got that first little idea, it's wonderful to get to share that with a crowd of 3,000 people."

Three thousand people? Actually, since playing to hundreds of people in the Bluebird Cafe, Taylor had graduated to arenas and stadiums. All over the world, her concerts sold out 20,000- to 40,000-seat venues! And all those people made her a better artist. "I feel like you have to push yourself in order to become a better performer, and I never want a fan to leave the show saying, 'That was just like the last tour.'" She told *Rolling Stone*, "At the end of the day, the sound of a screaming crowd is my favorite sound, and the sight of a sold-out stadium is my favorite view. Everything derives from that and revolves around making those people dance, sing along, feel like they aren't alone, and ultimately want to come back and see me the next time."

Dream Collaborator
"Jay Z . . . there could be something cool about that."

When Taylor isn't on the road, she tries to spend as much time at home as possible. However, home is more than one place for Taylor. Her estate in Watch Hill, Rhode Island, is where she loves to host all-girl parties for her and her besties to just laugh and have fun. Her

Taylor takes the Red Tour to her many Swifties Down Under.

house in Beverly Hills is mostly for when she has to spend time in the studio in Los Angeles. Her New York City apartment is for work and play . . . and shopping!

Of course, there is her Nashville **penthouse** apartment! That is her very favorite place of all. For the past couple of years, Taylor has enthusiastically described it in every interview. When she was furnishing it, she told *Rolling Stone*, "It's going to be my fantasy world. There's a pond in the living room, every cabinet in the kitchen is a different color, and today they're delivering a human-sized birdcage, which I'll put a brass telescope in. The ceiling of my living room is painted like the night sky. The pond is a moat around the fireplace and may possibly have koi fish in it, depending on my commitment.

"You step on a steppingstone in the pond in order to get on a spiral staircase, which takes you up to the human-sized birdcage."

Life isn't all fun and games for Taylor, though. Staying on top of the music business can be hard work. "The business aspect is one of the most important things about having a music career, because every choice you make in a management meeting affects your life a year-and-a-half from now," Taylor explained to *Billboard*.

"MY IDEA OF A GREAT SONG IS A SONG THAT SAYS HOW I FEEL, BETTER THAN I COULD."

Taylor's Nashville penthouse apartment. She overlooks the entire city.

Some of those business approvals have been **endorsement** deals. They include her fragrances, CoverGirl, Walgreens, Diet Coke, Target, American Greeting Cards, Keds, and many more. Besides the extra promotional work, Taylor added the big screen to her resume. First was *Valentine's Day* in 2010. Next she was the voice of Audrey in 2012's *The Lorax*.

Taylor's biggest role was Rosemary in the 2014 summer hit *The Giver*. No matter what toe-dipping she had been doing, music was still number one. In October 2014, she released her fifth album, *1989*. It was definitely a side step from her previous albums. *1989* was pure pop! Just before the release, Taylor told *Glamour* about the album, "It's already my favorite thing I've ever created." And when some country fans weren't happy with the change, Taylor explained, "I'm not trying to shed my skin. I'm trying to be a new version of the person I've been my whole life."

The first single, "Shake It Off," blasted out of the box. Quickly it was number one on the iTune and Hot 100

Vevo Views

"Shake It Off" got 8.3 million hits release day!

Taylor recording the voice of Audrey in *The Lorax*.

charts. The video featured Taylor as a hip-hop kid, ballerina, cheerleader, and more, but none of them really fit in.

"A lot of people who will relate to this song are people who are dealing with not ever feeling cool about themselves because other people make them feel like they don't fit in," she told a reporter. "One thing that I learned in this whole process is that you can get everything you want in life without ever feeling you fit in."

Lesson learned! And now she's teaching it!

Swiftie selfie! Taylor is there for her fans from eight to 80!

TAYLOR OPENS UP TO HER FANS

SHE TALKS ABOUT WORRYING, SONGWRITING, FRIENDSHIP, & MORE!

One thing everyone who knows Taylor Swift agrees on is that she is totally honest. What she thinks, she says—and writes about! She's gotten used to reporters and fans asking her questions, from "What do you do when you're not working?" to "What's your favorite dessert?" She handles questions with a smile and a thoughtful answer, and maybe even a recipe for her favorite chocolate chip cookies! Read on and you will see.

Swifties Unite

Taylor has more than 42 million Twitter followers.

On how she writes her songs . . . "I don't have any specific rituals and I've never written two songs the same way. An idea could hit you in the middle of the night, or you might say something in a conversation that would make a great lyric. I've written songs in airports, tour buses, hotel rooms, and on my bedroom floor. Writing songs is my way of dealing with love, feelings, and relationships."

On being a worrier . . . "I worry about everything. Future, past, present, where things are going, what I'm going to feel like in 20 years, what my life's going to be like, where I am going to live, where I am going to send my kids to school, what if there are paparazzi."

On paying attention to negative Internet gossip about her . . . "I know when not to read an article. Is it going to help my day? Is it important for my life? If the answer is no, then just don't click. . . . I'm careful about getting sucked into the rabbit hole that is the Internet because, as a songwriter, I don't have the option of having thick skin. As a writer you have to be open to everything, and that includes pain, rejection, self-doubt, fear. I deal with that enough on my own."

"MY FAVORITE HOBBY IS ANTIQUING . . . AT THE TENNESSEE STATE FAIR GROUNDS."

On her love of American music and history . . .
"I've been obsessed with fifties and sixties music, like the Shirelles and the Beach Boys. Like 'Wouldn't It Be

Nice'—if I ever had a wedding, I'd walk down the aisle to that song. . . . I read a 900-page book called *The Kennedy Women*, which goes back to the first Kennedy woman coming from Ireland in the 1800s. . . . I [also] bought books about John Adams, Lincoln's cabinet, the Founding Fathers, and Ellis Island."

On being nervous . . . "Lots of things still make me nervous: TV performances, heights, cynics. . . . I think fear can be a healthy motivator if you don't let it get out of control."

The Shirelles

The Beach Boys circa 1980s. (L to R): Al Jardine, Carl Wilson, Bruce Johnston, Brian Wilson, and Mike Love.

On what distracts her when performing . . .

"Sometimes I get really caught up in reading the signs, and if I get too caught up, I will start to read the signs when I'm singing, so I have to make sure I'm only reading signs in musical breaks. [The signs] are all pretty out there most of the time, which I like. There will be people who just make a giant, huge picture of my cat's face, so big that it's all I can see, and that usually gets my attention!"

On her friends . . . "My friends mean so much to me because they give me the opportunity to vent and complain about whatever I'm going through. They are also the people I want to celebrate with when things are

Pre-concert ritual: Taylor, her backup singers, dancers, and band all form a circle, touch hands, and cheer!

going well. . . . I need to talk to them before and after everything that happens to me."

On why she loves to read . . .

"It's fun to escape from where you are in your life and jump into somebody else's character. When you're reading a book, if you can really identify with one of the characters, it's like you can escape and go somewhere else. It's kind of like one of the thrills people get from going to the movies and seeing a story play out. But there's really nothing like reading. You can find such a quiet space and just kind of go to a different world."

On the nickname she never wants to be called again . . .

"When I was on the Brad Paisley tour, they called me Tater Tot. And the name on my dressing room was changed to Tater Swift every single day. It was like being teased by your big brother."

On her graduating high school . . .

"I [was] really excited because I didn't test out or get my GED. I actually went through the whole process of homeschooling. It was pretty tough doing it on the road, but I made it a priority and got my diploma in the mail."

People Person
Taylor was on the magazine's 40th anniversary cover.

TAYLOR LAND

A SUPER SWIFTIE SCRAPBOOK

FABULOUS FIRSTS

SONG SHE WROTE
"Lucky You"—she was 12

SONG SHE LEARNED TO PLAY ON THE GUITAR
The Dixie Chicks' "Cowboy Take Me Away"

ACTING ROLE
An episode of *CSI: Crime Scene Investigation*

HIT SONG
"Tim McGraw" from her first album, *Taylor Swift*

Tay and *Tonight Show*'s Jimmy Fallon laugh it up!

Shop Spot
"Antique stores are full of stories," says Tay.

SCHOOL DAYS

Taylor is the type of person who wants to share her good fortune with others—especially aspiring singer/songwriters. In October 2013, she opened the Taylor Swift Education Center, located at the Country Music Hall of Fame and Museum in Nashville. The school offers classes in songwriting, singing, musical instruments, and even dance. Her reason for the donation? "For Nashville to continue to be this hub for music and this hub for musical education," Taylor says.

TAYLOR'S B

Stevie Nicks: "[Taylor writes] songs that make the whole world sing, like Neil Diamond or Elton John. . . . Taylor's 'Today Was a Fairytale' has stayed in my heart forever. And it reminds me of me in a lot of ways."

Emma Stone: "She's so great! We're very different, but she has such a sick sense of humor. Nobody knows that. She's so great. People know . . . how hilarious she is. They've seen her on *SNL*. People are seeing it more now, and she's so funny and she's exactly who you think she is, and I love that."

Selena Gomez: "The difference between Taylor and me is she was 16 with the confidence of a 25-year-old. Actually, I should say 80-year-old, because she's such an old soul. I was not that way. I was very sheltered until about 18 or 19. . . . She does inspire me like crazy, but I wouldn't change my path, because it allowed me to figure out all that stuff and do it on my own."

ESTIES TALK

will.i.am: "Taylor Swift is dope. I'd like to work with Taylor Swift. I like the girl. We could do something really fantasy like. That would be cool."

Ed Sheeran: "Taylor writes songs in all different situations. I remember we went out . . . I think we were in the car to the studio and she took her phone out and mumbled something and sort of put it back. And I was like, 'What was that?' and she was like, 'Oh, I was just singing down ideas.'"

Lorde: "[Taylor has a] real teenage voice. . . . There are very few of us. The other teenagers sing other people's songs, which is fine, but it's not an authentic teenage experience."

DID YOU KNOW?

"Whenever I'm not on stage . . . I have glasses on. . . . I have a pair that are really, really wide, bifocally-looking. . . . They're the pair of glasses that no one recognizes me when I wear [them]. They're the pair of glasses that nobody was going to buy. They were really dusty and nobody wanted them. I felt bad for them, and I wear them everywhere. I bought them and gave them a nice home. I love them."

TAY TAY TRIVIA TIME

- Taylor named her first cat Meredith after the character Meredith Grey on *Grey's Anatomy*. She named her second cat Olivia after Olivia Benson on *Law & Order: SVU*.

- When Taylor had a Toyota car, she nicknamed it Toyoat.

- Magic 13—Taylor was born on December 13; her first album went gold in 13 weeks; her first number one song had a 13-second intro.

- One year Taylor gave homemade snow globes as Christmas presents. "I found out how to do it on Pinterest. It made for a lovely winter activity day—and it made me feel like a little kid again."

- The weirdest place she ever wrote a song? An airport bathroom! "I [grabbed] a paper towel and wrote lyrics on it. I still have it in a box in my room."

- Taylor is a talented painter. She loves painting watercolor flowers and portraits of her friends.

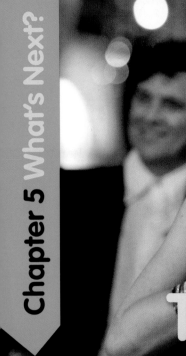

Taylor can't wait for whatever tomorrow will bring!

TAYLOR'S FUTURE TAKE
SHE'S MAKING HER DREAMS COME TRUE

"I think about my next move ten steps ahead," Taylor revealed to *Marie Claire*. "I'm always planning three award shows ahead. For me, planning is a productive way of stressing out about your life."

That's the professional Taylor Swift. Her hands-on approach to her career is well known. She knows when to concentrate on her musical career and when to spread her wings and try something different. That goes for business ventures, acting, and even taking time off.

As for acting, Taylor has already had a small taste. "Acting is something I've been fascinated by my entire life," she told OMG.Yahoo.com. And though she is constantly being sent scripts to read, she is looking for something special. Don't be surprised if you hear that Taylor is working on another film in the near future.

Of course, there are the small things she looks forward to. "I'd like to have a lot of friends," she counted off for *Glamour*. "I'd like to know how to make a good cup of tea. I'd like to have read a lot more classic books. I'd like to have a house with a fireplace. I'd like to be known as someone my friends can talk about their troubles with."

Those things seem like a given, but what about Taylor's personal life goals? "I've kind of realized that I have no idea where I'm going to be next year, or in six months, or in two months," she told *Wonderland*

> "I ALWAYS HAVE A TENDENCY TO WRITE A HAPPY ENDING TO MY STORY SONGS."

magazine. "I mean, I know where I'll be on tour in two months, but no idea where I'm going to be mentally, emotionally, dreams, goals, wishes, hopes. . . . daydreaming is wonderful, but you can never plan your future."

True, but never fear, Taylor will always be on top!

Resources

BOOK

Riley, Brooks. *Taylor Swift: The Story of Me.* New York: Scholastic, 2012.

ARTICLES

People, 40th Anniversary Issue October 2014
"Single and Loving It!"

Rolling Stone, September 25, 2014 issue
"The Reinvention of Taylor Swift"

Billboard, December 2, 2011
"Taylor Swift: Billboard's Woman of the Year"

Facts for Now

Visit this Scholastic Web site for more information on **Taylor Swift**: www.factsfornow.scholastic.com
Enter the keywords **Taylor Swift**

Glossary

endorsement *(en-DORS-muhnt)* support or approval of someone or something; famous people are often paid to endorse products

intern *(IN-turn)* someone who is learning a skill or job by working with an expert in that field

penthouse *(PENT-hous)* an apartment located on the top floor of a tall building

showcases *(SHOH-kase-iz)* special performances designed to draw attention to new musicians

Index

Academy of Country Music
    Award, 23
acting, 21, 22, 38, 45
Album of the Year Award, 23
American Music Award, 23

"Begin Again" single, 25
Best Country Album Award,
    23
Best Dressed of the Year
    Award, 25
Big Machine Records, 20
Billboard Music Awards, 24
birthday, 13, 43
Bluebird Cafe, 19, 27
Borchetta, Scott, 19–20

childhood, 6, 8–12, 14, 16–17
Cinnamon Twist (horse), 8
Country Music Association
    (CMA) Award, 23
Country Music Association
    (CMA) Music Festival, 20
Country Music Hall of Fame
    and Museum, 39
Creative Communications, 14
CSI: Crime Scene
    Investigation television
    show, 21, 38

distractions, 36
Dixie Chicks, The, 9, 38
education, 11–12, 16–17, 37, 39
endorsements, 30
"Everything Has Changed"
    single, 24, 25

Fact Files, 12–13, 14–15
fans, 13, 22, 27, 30, 33, 36
Fearless album, 20, 21, 23
friends, 13, 36–37, 43, 45

Giver, The movie, 30
glasses, 42

gossip, 34
Grammy Awards, 23

Hill, Faith, 9, 10, 23
history, 35
homes, 6, 11, 13, 16, 21, 23,
    27–29
humor, 40

"I Knew You Were Trouble"
    single, 25

karaoke, 11, 16

Lorax, The movie, 30
"Love Story" single, 23
"Lucky You" song, 16, 38

"Monster in My Closet"
    poem, 14

Nashville Songwriters
    Association, 23
Nashville, Tennessee, 10, 14,
    16, 17, 19, 21, 28, 39
nervousness, 35
Nickelodeon Kids' Choice
    Awards, 22
nicknames, 13, 37, 43

"Ours" song, 26

paintings, 8, 43
Paisley, Brad, 23, 37
pets, 13, 43
poetry, 14

"Read Every Day" Webcast,
    16
reading, 35, 37, 45
Red album, 24–25
"Red" single, 25
Rimes, LeAnn, 9–10
Rose, Liz, 22

Saturday Night Live television
    show, 20, 22, 40
"Shake It Off" single, 25,
    30–31
Sheeran, Ed, 19, 24, 41
shyness, 12, 26
snow globes, 43
Songwriter Artist of the Year
    Award, 23
Speak Now album, 23–24,
    26
Swift, Andrea (mother), 6, 8,
    11, 14, 17, 20, 21
Swift, Austin (brother), 6, 8,
    11, 20
Swift, Scott (father), 6, 8, 11,
    20

Taylor Swift album, 20, 22, 38
Taylor Swift Education Center,
    39
Teen Choice Awards, 21, 23
"Tim McGraw" single, 20,
    21, 38
"Today Was a Fairytale"
    single, 40
tours, 20, 27, 37
"22" single, 25
Twitter, 13, 33

Valentine's Day movie, 22,
    23, 30
videos, 25, 31

"We Are Never Ever Getting
    Back Together" single, 25
worry, 34
writing, 12, 14, 16–17, 19, 22,
    24, 25–27, 33–34, 38, 39,
    40, 41, 43, 45

"You Belong To Me" single,
    22

Acknowledgments

Page 3: Advice: *Glamour* March 2014
Page 6: Magical childhood: *Rolling Stone* March 5, 2009
Page 8: Finger paints: *Rolling Stone* October 25, 2012; Encouragement: *Cosmopolitan* UK January 2013; Annoying kid: *CosmoGirl* December/January 2009
Page 9: *Lion King: Marie Claire* June 2012; Confidence: Seventeen.com
Page 10: Freaked out: *Philadelphia Style* Summer 2011; Nashville: *CosmoGirl* December/January 2009
Page 11: Karaoke: *Rolling Stone* March 5, 2009; Middle school: *Vogue* February 2012
Page 12: Didn't fit in: *Vogue* February 2012
Page 14: Tangled-haired kid: *People* January 14, 2011
Page 16: Writing songs: *TeenVogue* March 2009; Sounds like a chipmunk:

Scholastic Live Webcast 2013; Superpower: *M* magazine
Page 17: Mean girls: *Rolling Stone* March 5, 2009; *InStyle*
Page 19: Bluebird Cafe: *Allure* April 2009
Page 20: Junior High: *Allure* April 2009
Page 21: "Tim McGraw": *Billboard* October 23, 2010
Page 26: Song writing: *Rolling Stone* February 4, 2012; Songs are stories: VH1 NEWS October 17, 2012
Page 27: Push yourself: *Rolling Stone* August 1, 2013; Dream Collaborator: *Ladies Home Journal* 2011
Page 28: Penthouse apartment: *Rolling Stone* February 4, 2010
Page 29: Business: *Billboard* December 10, 2011
Page 30: Shed my skin: *Glamour* March 2014
Page 33: Writing songs: *Dolly* 2013

Page 34: Worrier: *Glamour* November 2012; Internet gossip: *Glamour* March 2014; American music: *Rolling Stone* August 1, 2013; Ladies home Journal.com 2013; Antiquing/hobby: Nashville Lifestyles.com
Page 35: Nervous: *Teen Vogue*
Page 36: Distractions: *Rolling Stone* August 1, 2013; Friends: *Cosmopolitan* UK January 2013
Page 37: Reading: Scholastic Webcast October 2012; Nickname: *Time* October 19, 2012; GED: Just Jared Jr. November 11, 2008
Page 39: School Days: *The Tennessean* October 9, 2013; Antique Stores: Nashville Lifestyles.com
Page 40: Stevie Nicks: Time.com April 29, 2010; Emma

Stone: MTV News April 5, 2010; Selena Gomez: *TeenVogue* December/January 2014
Page 41: Will.i.am: Capitalfm.com July 12, 2013; Ed Sheeran MTV News September 21, 2012; Lorde: People.com January 23, 2014
Page 42: Glasses: *OK!* October 8, 2008
Page 43: Snow globes: *People* December 2011; Airport bathroom: MTV News February 13, 2012
Page 44: Next move: *Marie Claire* July 2012
Page 45: Acting: OMG.Yahoo.com March 1, 2012; Friends: *Glamour* March 2014; Where she will be: *Wonderland* Summer 2013, Happy Ending: *InStyle* June 2011

About the Author

Marie Morreale is the author of many official and unofficial celebrity biographies. She attended New York University as an English/creative writing major and began her writing and editorial career in New York City. As the editor of teen/music magazines *Teen Machine* and *Jam!*, she covered TV, film, and music personalities and interviewed superstars such as Michael Jackson, Britney Spears, and Justin Timberlake/*NSYNC. Morreale was also an editor/writer at Little Golden Books.

Today, she is the executive editor, Media, of Scholastic Classroom Magazines writing about pop-culture, sports, news, and special events. Morreale lives in New York City and is entertained daily by her two Maine coon cats, Cher and Sullivan.